HÄGAR THE HORRIBLE

BRINGS 'EM BACK ALIVE!

HÄGAR THE HORRIBLE

BRINGS 'EM BACK ALIVE!

by Dik Browne

tempo books
GROSSET & DUNLAP
A FILMWAYS COMPANY
Publishers • New York

Hagar the Horrible Brings 'Em Back Alive

ISBN: 0-448-14327-5
A Tempo Books Original
Tempo Books is registered in the U.S. Patent Office
Published simultaneously in Canada
Printed in the United States of America

IT'S THE GREAT WALL OF EUROPE— BUILT TO KEEP OUT THE BARBARIANS
GOOD IDEA!
DIK BROWNE 6-27
WHO BUILT IT?
I DUNNO.... THE PEOPLE ON THE OTHER SIDE
© King Features Syndicate, Inc., 1977.

BOY! THAT SMELLS GOOD!
EVERYTHING SMELLS GOOD TO YOU
7-12

NO, REALLY— WHAT IS IT?
I'M BOILING AN EGG
© King Features Syndicate, Inc., 1977.
DIK BROWNE

DON'T LIE TO ME! YOU KNOW CREAMED OYSTERS ARE A NO-NO!
I, ER...
© King Features Syndicate, Inc., 1977.
AND SO ARE PICKLED CHERRIES!
SHE'S SPOOKY!
HOW DID YOU KNOW?
MEN WITH BEARDS HAVE NO SECRETS
3-30
DIK BROWNE

THAT DRINKING FOUNTAIN FOR THE GUYS WAS A GREAT IDEA!
DRINKING FOUNTAIN?
© King Features Syndicate, Inc., 1977.

HELP! THE SHIP IS SINKING!!
6-17
DIK BROWNE

© King Features Syndicate, Inc., 1977.
World rights reserved.
≡SIGH≡ DON'T TELL ME IT'S SPRING AGAIN!
3-29
DIK BROWNE

THIS @*!!%.. COUNTRY IS GETTING SOFT!
WE ARE NOT!!!

NOT YOU, STUPID! I SAID THIS COUNTRY IS GETTING SOFT!
3-28
DIK BROWNE

HAGAR
YOU OVERDO EVERYTHING! STOP EATING THOSE CHERRIES!
OKAY

DIK BROWNE 6-6
© King Features Syndicate, Inc., 1977. World rights reserved.
AND GET RID OF THOSE CHERRY PITS!

WHAT'S WRONG WITH HAGAR?
NOTHING. HIS FOOT'S ASLEEP
THUMP!
BAM!
BOOM!
DIK BROWNE 6-10
© King Features Syndicate, Inc., 1977.

BOY! I'D HATE TO HAVE HIM WAKE ME UP!
SLOSH!
BAM!

DO YOU HAVE TO PLAY WITH THAT STUPID TOY ?!!
ZAP ZAP
NOW, NOW, HONI, REMEMBER– YOU'RE ONLY A KID ONCE
© King Features Syndicate, Inc., 1976.
USUALLY
ZAP ZAP
9-10 DIK BROWNE

LISTEN! IT WON'T HURT YOU TO SPEND A DAY WITH YOUR FAMILY ON THE BEACH
AW!

AW!
AW!
AW!
AH!!
9-11
DIK BROWNE
© King Features Syndicate, Inc., 1976.

THEY'RE GETTING BIGGER—THEY SHOULD HAVE THEIR OWN ROOM
THE KIDS *HAVE* THEIR OWN ROOMS

DIK BROWNE 7-21
© King Features Syndicate, Inc., 1977.
I MEAN THE ANIMALS

THE FAUCET'S LEAKING
SO WHAT?
DRIP
DRIP
DRIP
© King Features Syndicate, Inc., 1977. World rights reserved.
YIIIIPE!!!
WHY DIDN'T YOU SAY IT WAS MY FAUCET?
DIK BROWE 4-16
XXX

GO, SNERT! FETCH!!
© King Features Syndicate, Inc., 1976.
I'M AFRAID YOU'RE NOT MUCH OF A RETRIEVER...
YOU'RE PRETTY GOOD WITH THE LADIES THOUGH
DIK BROWNE 9-9

I BRING GOOD NEWS
© King Features Syndicate, Inc., 1977. World rights reserved.
DIK BROWNE 4-7
WELL, THEY DO SAY "NO NEWS IS GOOD NEWS"

FOR MY RECORDS, WHAT ILLNESSES HAVE YOU HAD?
LEMME SEE
© King Features Syndicate, Inc., 1976.
BLACK PLAGUE... EVIL EYE... DEMON POSSESSION ...SPELLS
I'LL JUST PUT DOWN "REGULAR CHILDHOOD DISEASES"
DIK BROWNE 9-8

THIS IS THE "SINGING SWORD OF ANTIOCH"
REALLY?
DIK BROWNE
4-1

LISTEN...
COME TO ME MY MELANCHOLY BABY...

WHAT A BEAUTIFUL POEM!
WHAT'S IT ABOUT?
© King Features Syndicate, Inc., 1977.
AN INNOCENT FARM BOY'S BITTER ENCOUNTER WITH THE REAL WORLD, IN WHICH HE YEARNS FOR THE GOOD THINGS BUT HAS NO MONEY!
WOW! WHAT IS IT CALLED?
SIMPLE SIMON
DIK BROWNE 4-15

AFTER THE WINTER EVERYTHING SMELLS MUSTY
I'M GOING TO PUT EVERYTHING OUT TO AIR
GOOD IDEA

NEXT, I'M GOING TO DO THE FURNITURE
4-6.
DIK BROWNE
© King Features Syndicate, Inc., 1977.

IN MY DAY KIDS HAD TO GROW UP FAST!
© King Features Syndicate, Inc., 1976.
HOW OLD ARE YOU?
13, SIR
WHEN I WAS YOUR AGE I WAS 20
DIK BROWNE 10-26

HAGAR! YOU'VE GOT TO DO SOMETHING ABOUT THESE DRAGONS!
LISTEN— YOU'RE THE ONE WHO WANTED TO MOVE TO THE SUBURBS!
7-11
BROWNE
© King Features Syndicate, Inc., 1977. World rights reserved.

DO YOU REMEMBER THE MAID MARION WHO WAS CARRIED OFF BY SVEN THE BOLD?
OF COURSE
ISN'T THAT HER DAUGHTER?
I THINK IT IS...
TIMES SURE ARE CHANGING
DIK BROWNE 7-1
© King Features Syndicate, Inc., 1977. World rights reserved.

IF YOU WANNA TRAIN THAT PUP – THE FIRST THING IS TO SHOW HIM WHO THE BOSS IS!
RIGHT!

© King Features Syndicate, Inc., 1977.
DIK BROWNE 4-14
BOSS
BOSS
NOW, WHAT'S THE SECOND THING?

I HEAR THE ENEMY! NOW BARE YOUR STEEL AND BANISH MERCY!
AND LET THIS BE OUR BATTLE CRY—
DIK BROWNE 6-30
"LIVE AND LET LIVE"
© King Features Syndicate, Inc., 1977.

I'M NOT GOING TO WEAR THESE STUPID THINGS ON MY HORNS!

OKAY— THEN YOU GOTTA SLEEP IN THE UPPER BUNK!
DIK BROWNE 4-13
© King Features Syndicate, Inc., 1977. World rights reserved.

HURRY UP AND WAIT! HURRY UP AND WAIT!
THAT'S THE ARMY FOR YOU!!
ZAP!

I SURE HOPE THOSE LADDERS GET HERE SOON!
4-12
DIK BROWNE
© King Features Syndicate, Inc., 1977.

HE ATE THEM!
NO!! HOW DID YOU GET DADDY TO EAT BRUSSELS SPROUTS?!
DIK BROWNE 4-11
© King Features Syndicate, Inc., 1977.

I TOLD HIM THEY WERE GREEN MEATBALLS

SOMETIMES I WISH I WEREN'T A VIKING!
© King Features Syndicate, Inc., 1977.
IF YOU WEREN'T, YOU'D PROBABLY BE STUCK ON SOME CRUMMY FARM WITH A NAGGING WIFE, BAWLING KIDS, UP TO YOUR NECK IN DEBT —THEN WHERE WOULD YOU BE ?!!
HOME...
3-31
BROWNE

GO SEEK A HUSBAND WHERE HEROES DWELL... CAMELOT ...AVALON...
© King Features Syndicate, Inc., 1976. World rights reserved.
HEY, YOU DON'T HAVE TO GO THAT FAR! YOUR MOTHER MET ME RIGHT HERE...
TRY RUSSIA... SEE IF PERSIA IS STILL OPEN...
8-27 DIK BROWNE

WHY ARE MOTHS ATTRACTED TO FLAMES, DAD?
IT ISN'T THE FLAMES— THEY LIKE CANDLES
© King Features Syndicate, Inc., 1977.
THEY LIKE CANDLES?
SURE, THEY EAT CANDLES
DIK BROWNE 6-29
SEE?

CAMELOT! MY DREAM CASTLE! ISN'T IT ROMANTIC?
I DUNNO...
© King Features Syndicate, Inc., 1977.

I'LL BET IT COSTS A FORTUNE TO HEAT
4-30 DIK BROWNE

I HEAR HAGAR BROUGHT YOU HOME A WORK OF ART...
BIG DEAL

LIKE EVERYTHING HE BRINGS HOME— IT'S BROKEN!
DIK BROWNE
5-7
© King Features Syndicate, Inc., 1977.

I THOUGHT YOU LIKED THE LOOTING BUSINESS
I DO — BUT THE OVERHEAD IS KILLING ME —
WHAT OVERHEAD?
BONK!
OH...
5-6
DIK BROWNE
© King Features Syndicate, Inc., 1977.

KIDS TODAY! YETCH!!
NOW, NOW...
REMEMBER– YOU WERE YOUNG ONCE YOURSELF...
© King Features Syndicate Inc. 1977 World rights reserved
ONCE?! I WAS YOUNG LOTSA TIMES!!!
DIK BROWNE 4-29

OH, NO! IT'S GONE!!
HAGAR! DID YOU TAKE THE CRUMB CAKE?
DIK BROWNE 4-25
WHAT CRUMB CAKE?
© King Features Syndicate, Inc., 1977. World rights reserved.

EACH NIGHT THE SUN SINKS INTO THE SEA AND THE WATER PUTS OUT THE FIRE...
BUT, DAD—THAT'S JUST A MYTH!
DIK BROWNE 4-18
SSSSSS

© King Features Syndicate, Inc., 1977. World rights reserved.
BONK!
NAME DROPPER!!!
CORBINO
5-5 DIK BROWNE

WHY DO VIKINGS WEAR HORNS, DAD?
I'LL TELL YOU IF YOU PROMISE NOT TO TELL YOUR MOTHER - - -
DIK BROWNE 9-5
THEY'RE REALLY EAR PLUGS.

LOOK, HAGAR — A SAXON!
SO WHAT?
IF YOU'VE SEEN ONE, YOU'VE SEEN THEM ALL
NOT QUITE...
5-14 DIK BROWNE
© King Features Syndicate, Inc., 1977.

IS IT JUST ME, OR
IS IT COLD IN HERE?
DIK BROWNE 5-12
© King Features Syndicate, Inc., 1977. World rights reserved.

HURRY UP! CAST OFF! GET SAILING!
I JUST HAD AN ARGUMENT WITH HELGA, AND BELIEVE IT OR NOT...
I FINALLY GOT IN THE LAST WORD!
DIK BROWNE 9-7
©King Features Syndicate, Inc., 1973. World rights reserved.

MEN WORK TILL SETTING SUN, BUT WOMAN'S WORK IS NEVER DONE!
DIK BROWNE
5-10
© King Features Syndicate, Inc., 1977.
THAT'S BECAUSE OF POOR ORGANIZATION

AT'S HAT?
IT'S A NEW ENGLISH INVENTION– AN EGG SANDWICH
IT'S A SLICE OF BREAD BETWEEN TWO FRIED EGGS
© King Features Syndicate, Inc., 1977.
4-28
DIK BROWNE
...OF COURSE, IT ISN'T PERFECTED YET...

I HAVE A MESSAGE FOR HAGAR THE HORRIBLE —HERO OF THE VIKINGS— HAVE YOU SEEN HIM?
YOU'RE LOOKING AT HIM, PAL!
1-5
DIK BROWNE

NO! I MEAN SERIOUSLY!
©King Features Syndicate, Inc., 1973.

SNEAKING IN AFTER MIDNIGHT, EH?
© King Features Syndicate, Inc., 1977. World rights reserved.
REMEMBER—IF YOU TELL A LIE YOUR HORNS WILL FALL OFF!
5-4
DIK BROWNE
WAIT FOR THE QUESTION! WAIT FOR THE QUESTION!!

SIGN THE PEACE TREATY!
© King Features Syndicate, Inc., 1977.
HEY! WE GOT THE SAME NAME!
DIK BROWNE 4-27

TO THE VICTORS!!
BOY! THE ENGLISH ARE GOOD SPORTS!
NOT REALLY... THAT'S POISON IVY
DIK BROWNE 4-26

BOY! THIS IS TERRIBLE!
I WONDER WHAT'S WRONG?

MAYBE IT'S THE NEW SAIL...
© King Features Syndicate, Inc., 1977.
8-27
DIK BROWNE

WHAT DID DADDY BRING YOU?
JUST A FANCY TEAPOT
© King Features Syndicate, Inc., 1977.

MY MAGIC LAMP!
DIK BROWNE 8-26

DO YOU HAVE MOLES?
NO, WHY?

THEN GET READY FOR A SURPRISE ATTACK!
© King Features Syndicate, Inc., 1977.
DIK BROWNE 8-25

WHAT DID YOU GET D-A-D-D-Y FOR HIS B-I-R-T-H-D-A-Y?
A NICE H-U-N-T-I-N-G K-N-I-F-E

BOY! I HATE IT WHEN THEY SPELL THINGS!
8-24
DIK BROWNE
© King Features Syndicate, Inc., 1977.

OH! WHO LEFT THAT DOOR OPEN AGAIN?!!
5-3
© King Features Syndicate, Inc., 1977. World rights reserved.

WHAT'LL YOU HAVE?
WHATCHA GOT?
I GOT GIN, SCOTCH, VODKA, RYE, RUM, BOURBON, BEER, ALE, WINE, BRANDY
OKAY, THAT'LL BE FINE
DIK BROWNE - 8-23

IN THIS WORLD YOU GOTTA LOOK OUT FOR NUMBER ONE!
DIK BROWNE-8-22
© King Features Syndicate, Inc., 1977.
WHAT DOES HE LOOK LIKE?

©King Features Syndicate, Inc., 1973.
LOOK, HONI! I BROUGHT YOU A SUITOR!
SAY 'HELLO' TO THE LADY!
DIK BROWNE
DARN IT! HE GOT AWAY!
10-19

INDIA'S A LOVELY COUNTRY BUT I'M GLAD WE'RE GOING HOME
© King Features Syndicate, Inc., 1977. World rights reserved.

IT'LL BE GOOD TO SLEEP IN MY OWN BED AGAIN
DIK BROWNE
7-9

AT LAST! YOU FINALLY BROUGHT ME SOMETHING I CAN USE!

≷SIGH≶... AND TO THINK I CARTED THAT DRINKING MUG ALL OVER EUROPE!
DIK BROWNE 9-10
©King Features Syndicate, Inc., 1973.

BOY! I GOT HEARTBURN!
THAT ISN'T WHERE YOUR HEART IS

THAT'S WHERE HAGAR'S HEART IS!
7-8 DIK BROWNE
© King Features Syndicate, Inc., 1977.

BAM!
BONK!
SLASH!
USE NEXT WINDOW
@☆!!... IT HAPPENS EVERY TIME!
© King Features Syndicate, Inc., 1978. World rights reserved.
9-7

I WISH THAT JUST ONCE YOU'D ADMIT YOU WERE WRONG!
DIK BROWNE
7-7

OKAY— OKAY— SO I MADE A WRONG TURN!

WELL, DON'T JUST SIT THERE! GO SEE WHAT THEY WANT!
DIK BROWNE
5-9
© King Features Syndicate, Inc., 1977.

DRAT! DARN SHOE-LACES!
© King Features Syndicate, Inc., 1977.

I HEREBY KNIGHT THEE BARON OF KITCH AND SUCH AND SUCH!
DIK BROWNE 6-28

BOY! TALK ABOUT BEING IN THE RIGHT PLACE AT THE RIGHT TIME!

YOU GUYS JUST VOTED TO GIVE ME A BIGGER SHARE
© King Features Syndicate, Inc., 1977.

WHEN ?
WE DIDN'T HEAR ANYTHING ABOUT A VOTE!!
NATURALLY

DIK BROWNE 7-6
IT WAS A SECRET BALLOT

YOU FRENCH ARE OKAY BUT YOU DON'T KNOW HOW TO DRINK...
© King Features Syndicate, Inc., 1977.

THE DIFFERENCE BETWEEN YOU AND ME IS I KNOW WHEN I'VE HAD ENOUGH!
DIK BROWNE 7-5

...5,...6...7...8...9...10!
THANKS
7-4 DIK BROWNE -
HOW COULD DOING THAT MAKE YOUR STOMACH SMALLER?
I DUNNO... DR. ZOOK TOLD ME TO TOUCH MY TOES 10 TIMES A DAY AND IT WOULD
© King Features Syndicate, Inc., 1977.

WHO DID YOU WANT TO SEE?
DIK BROWNE 6-4

COMO UZU DA POPO LALA
BONO BONO
WHAT'S HE SAYING?
GOOD NEWS! THIS ISN'T QUICKSAND!
OH, GOOD!
IT'S CEMENT
DIK BROWNE 9-6
© King Features Syndicate, Inc., 1976.

HALT! WHO GOES THERE—FRIEND OR FOE?
FRIEND!
6-3
DIK BROWNE
OKAY, ADVANCE
1977 World rights reserved
WOW! YOU ARE A FRIEND!
King Features Syndicate, Inc.

THIS FLOWER LOOKS FUNNY...
DID YOU WATER IT EVERY DAY LIKE I TOLD YOU?
YEAH, SORTA...
HIC!
DIK BROWNE
6-2

BOY! I'LL BE GLAD WHEN THIS OIL SHORTAGE IS OVER!
DIK BROWNE
© King Features Syndicate, Inc., 1977. 5-31

I WONDER WHAT TIME IT IS!
SHH...

DIK BROWNE
5-30
© King Features Syndicate, Inc., 1977. World rights reserved.

SNACK TIME!
BONG!

OH, YES, WE ALWAYS HAVE A BIG TREE FOR CHRISTMAS...
12-25
DIK BROWNE
© King Features Syndicate, Inc., 1976.

HAGAR SURE HAS THE CHRISTMAS SPIRIT
DIK BROWNE 12-24
© King Features Syndicate, Inc., 1976. World rights reserved.

ONE OF THE MOST BEAUTIFUL AND SACRED MOMENTS OF A WOMAN'S LIFE IS WHEN THE RIGHT MAN PROPOSES.

TREAT IT WITH GREAT DIGNITY...

SO DON'T GO YELLING "GOTCHA!"
DIK BROWNE

NOW WE'LL TEST YOUR REFLEXES...
6-1

REFLEXES GOOD

BUT, HAGAR— THERE ARE TOO MANY!
NONSENSE! I LOVE TO FIGHT AGAINST INSANE ODDS!
© King Features Syndicate, Inc., 1977.
AS LONG AS THEY'RE *REASONABLY* INSANE ODDS
3-11
DIK BROWNE

© King Features Syndicate, Inc., 1976.
THIS IS THE MOST IMPORTANT PART OF THE PLAN...
SO LISTEN CLOSELY!
DIK BROWNE
12-31

HELGA! WE'RE HAVING FISH TONIGHT! GET SOME WHITE WINE...
© King Features Syndicate, Inc., 1978.

AS A MATTER OF FACT— GET LOTS OF WHITE WINE!!
DIK BROWNE
12-22

TODAY WE'RE SERVING THE CREW GREASE BALL DUCK
BUT THEY LOOK LIKE REGULAR GREASE BALLS...
© King Features Syndicate, Inc., 1976.
WHY DO YOU CALL THEM *DUCK*?
12-30
DIK BROWNE

YAH! YAH! YOU COULDN'T HIT ME WITH A SNOWBALL!
© King Features Syndicate, Inc., 1976.

OH, YEAH!!
DIK BROWNE 1-1

HOW DO YOU EXPECT TO CONQUER THE WORLD WHEN YOU CAN'T EVEN MASTER YOURSELF?
JUST ASK YOURSELF THAT!
© King Features Syndicate, Inc., 1977.
BECAUSE I'M A MUCH TOUGHER CUSTOMER, THAT'S WHY!
2-19
DIK BROWNE

I'M AFRAID THIS MIGHT HURT YOU!
HURRY UP, AND DON'T WORRY!
©King Features Syndicate, Inc., 1973. World rights reserved.

IT COULDN'T HURT AS MUCH AS HELGA.
DIK BROWNE 9-8
COOKIES

STUPID! DON'T YOU KNOW THAT'S THE WORST THING YOU CAN DO FOR A BAD BACK?!!

HEY! LOOK WHAT I FOUND IN MY OYSTER!
DIK BROWNE
THERE'S ONE IN MINE, TOO!
I'D BETTER THROW THEM OUT! THEY'RE PROBABLY ALL LIKE THAT!
9-4
©King Features Syndicate, Inc., 1973. World rights reserved.

WHERE ARE WE ?
I DON'T KNOW. I'LL ASK IN THIS PLACE.
Ye Pig and Whistle
© King Features Syndicate, Inc., 1975.
ZAP! ZAP! ZAP! ZAP!
NEVER TAKE ANYTHING THAT LOOKS LIKE A DARTBOARD INTO AN ENGLISH PUB !
12-27
DIK BROWNE

TAKE THE DOG FOR A WALK
AW, DO I HAVE TO?
© King Features Syndicate, Inc., 1975. World rights reserved.
LISTEN! A LITTLE WALK WON'T HURT YOU!
YEAH, BUT HE'S HEAVY!
DIK BROWNE 12-26

NO–YOU SHOULD HAVE TURNED LEFT AT TURKEY.
12-25
DIK BROWNE

YOU OVERDO EVERYTHING
YOU CAN'T JUST HAVE A YULE LOG

YOU HAVE TO HAVE THE *BIGGEST!*
12-24
DIK BROWNE-
© King Features Syndicate, Inc., 1975. World rights reserved.

HELGA SAYS YOU HAVE TO WASH BEFORE YOU COME TO DINNER.
I DID.

NOT JUST YOUR HANDS!
DIK BROWNE 12-23
© King Features Syndicate, Inc., 1975. World rights reserved.

I GOT THE NEW ANCHOR.
GOOD! NOW DON'T LOSE THIS ONE!

DON'T WORRY. IT'S MADE OF CORK— IT FLOATS
12-22
DIK BROWNE
© King Features Syndicate, Inc., 1975. World rights reserved.

SLASH!
HAW! HAW!

SPLF...
SPLF ?!

DARN! MY WIFE'S BEEN USING MY BLADE ON HER LEGS AGAIN!
10-23
DIK BROWNE

GRANDPA, YOU ARE SO OLD YOU MUST BE FULL OF WISDOM...
OH, YES, YES
© King Features Syndicate, Inc., 1976.

IT MUST BE WONDERFUL TO HAVE ALL THAT WISDOM AND INSIGHT...
OH, YES, YES

BUT I'D RATHER HAVE TEETH
DIK BROWNE
10-21

HEY! HERE COMES THE LORD MAYOR OF LONDON
PEACE, HAGAR! I BRING YOU THE KEYS TO THE CITY
© King Features Syndicate, Inc., 1976. World rights reserved.

HOW ABOUT THAT ?! PRETTY GOOD, EH?
WAS THAT WISE, M'LORD ?

I THINK SO...THOSE WERE THE KEYS TO BIRMINGHAM
DIK BROWNE 10-22

THE TIME HAS COME FOR REAL MEN TO STAND UP AND BE COUNTED!
YEAH!
RIGHT ON!
DIK BROWNE 10-20
© King Features Syndicate, Inc., 1976. World rights reserved.
GOOD... NOW, CAN ANYBODY HERE COUNT?

I'M NOT JUST LOOKING FOR A HUSBAND
I WANT TO GET A MAN WHO IS STRONG BUT SOFT. BRAVE BUT WISE. SOBER, DEPENDABLE, FUNNY, CONSIDERATE
DIK BROWNE
© King Features Syndicate, Inc., 1976. World rights reserved.
GET TWO
10-19

WELL, IT'S GOOD FOR THE CROPS
WHAT ARE YOU RAISING?
© King Features Syndicate, Inc., 1976. World rights reserved.

FROZEN PEAS
10-18
DIK BROWNE

IS THAT A BIRD BATH?
NAW
© King Features Syndicate, Inc., 1977.

IT WAS GONNA BE A STATUE OF HAGAR, BUT WE RAN OUT OF MONEY
HÄG
DIKBROWNE
6-14

HAGAR! COME EAT BEFORE YOUR DINNER GETS HOT!
© King Features Syndicate, Inc., 1977. World rights reserved.
HOT?
WE'RE HAVING COLD CUTS
6-13

THIS DAY I'VE FOUGHT A DOZEN BATTLES AGAINST A HUNDRED FOES...SUFFERED SLINGS AND ARROWS JUST TO REACH HOME...
AND NOW YOU TELL ME...
© King Features Syndicate, Inc., 1977.

WE'RE GOING OUT TONIGHT?!
HURRY UP AND CHANGE
6-25
DIK BROWNE

WHERE DO YOU WANT ME TO RUB ?
WHERE IT HURTS... IN THE SMALL OF MY BACK –
DIK BROWNE 6-24

I DON'T THINK THERE IS A SMALL OF *YOUR* BACK!

WHERE DO YOU WANT IT?
?
© King Features Syndicate, Inc., 1977.

WANT WHAT?
SVEN! LOOK! SOMEBODY STOLE THE RUG!
DIK BROWNE 6-23

DO YOU SOMETIMES FEEL THAT THE WHOLE WORLD IS AGAINST YOU?

SOMETIMES...
6-22
DIK BROWNE

WHO WAS THAT FRESH OLD MAN?
© King Features Syndicate, Inc., 1977. World rights reserved.

IGNORE HIM! THAT'S KING LEER!
6-21 DIK BROWNE

BUT HOW COULD THEY DO IT ?!
OH, IT'S A COMMON ENOUGH MISTAKE...
© King Features Syndicate, Inc., 1977.
6
DIK BROWNE
6-20

THEY JUST READ THE PLANS UPSIDE DOWN

WE'LL EAT AS SOON AS DADDY GETS HOME WITH OUR DINNER
I'M HOME, DEAR
7-2 DIK BROWNE
DID YOU BRING THE CHICKEN?
DRAT! I KNEW IT WAS SOMETHING LIKE THAT!
© King Features Syndicate, Inc., 1977.

IT'S NOT THE EDGE OF THE WORLD! IT'S JUST A WATERFALL!
OH, GOOD!
DIK BROWNE
4-2

I THOUGHT WE WERE IN TROUBLE!
© King Features Syndicate, Inc., 1977.

HAGAR'S VERY TOUCHY TODAY
AW, HE'S OKAY...

DON'T STEP ON MY SHADOW, STUPID!
BOY! THAT'S TOUCHY!
© King Features Syndicate, Inc., 1977.
7-26
DIK BROWNE

I AIN'T GONNA WASH ARROWS! THAT'S A STUPID ORDER!
OH, YEAH?! I'LL TEACH YOU!!
GO STAND IN THE CORNER!
THAT'S ANOTHER STUPID ORDER!
7-13
DIK BROWNE

WHEN YOU'RE MARRIED, YOU SHOULDN'T REPEAT THINGS A HUNDRED TIMES TO YOUR HUSBAND... JUST SAY IT ONCE — LIKE THIS—
GET UP!!
© King Features Syndicate, Inc., 1977.
MEN DON'T LIKE WOMEN WHO NAG
7-14
DIK BROWNE

DO ALL VIKINGS WEAR HORNS?
NAW, JUST IMPORTANT ONES
THE BIGGER THE HORNS, THE MORE IMPORTANT
© King Features Syndicate, Inc.,
OH, THIS IS MY WIFE HELGA
DIK BROWNE
7-16

THERE'S AN AWFUL LOT OF VIKINGS AT SERVICE TONIGHT
THAT SIGN WAS A MISTAKE

THE GREATEST SIN!
TONIGHT
IT SHOULD HAVE SAID "WORST"
5-17
DIK BROWNE
© King Features Syndicate, Inc., 1977.

WE'RE PLAYING BRIDGE WITH THE HANSSENS TONIGHT...
OH, DRAT!
OH, STOP IT! YOU KNOW YOU LOVE TO PLAY BRIDGE!
LONDON BRIDGE IS FALLING DOWN...
DIK BROWNE 5-18

WHERE'S MY COMB AND BRUSH ?!
HAGAR! DID YOU TAKE MY...
DIK BROWNE 7-27
OH, NEVER MIND...
© King Features Syndicate, Inc., 1977. World rights reserved.

TRY TO GET A WAITER

NOT LIKE THAT, STUPID!
DIK BROWNE 7-25
© King Features Syndicate, Inc., 1977. World rights reserved.

I GO TO FIND GLORY!
BUT REMEMBER...
DIK BROWNE 8-6
BEHIND EVERY GREAT MAN IS A WOMAN!
© King Features Syndicate, Inc., 1977.
I KNOW... PICKING UP AFTER HIM —

HOW WAS THE VIKING FEAST?
FANTASTIC!
THERE WAS SO MUCH FOOD I COULDN'T FINISH IT ALL!
BUT I TOOK HOME A 'DOGGIE BAG'
© King Features Syndicate, Inc., 1977.
8-5
DIK BROWNE

HAGAR—
WOULD YOU
LIKE TO
SEE A
TRICK?
I'M
VERY
BUSY

OH, OKAY... BUT IT BETTER BE
GOOD!!
DIK
BROWNE
8-4

DADDY, WHERE DO THE STARS GO IN THE DAYTIME?
ITALY
ITALY?
© King Features Syndicate, Inc.,
8-2
YOUR FATHER THINKS EVERYBODY WOULD GO TO ITALY IF THEY HAD THE CHANCE

SONNY, THAT'S DEADLY QUICKSAND! AREN'T YOU WORRIED?
NAW
© King Features Syndicate, Inc., 1977.

I JUST LIVE ONE DAY AT A TIME...
8-3 DIK BROWNE

LAND HO!
DIK BROWNE 8-1
© King Features Syndicate, Inc., 1977.

A FUNNY
WAY OF
FIGHTING
WHAT'S THAT ?
ZAP!
ZAP!
ZAP!
THEY ALWAYS TRY TO KILL THE LEADER FIRST
THAT IS FUNNY
10-30 DIK BROWNE
© King Features Syndicate, Inc., 1976.
ZAP
ZAP

THEY'RE GONE!!
HAGAR! WHAT DID YOU DO WITH THE DOUGHNUTS ?!

DIK BROWNE 10-29
WHAT DOUGHNUTS ?
© King Features Syndicate, Inc., 1976.

NOW
HY I LIKE
VODKA?
NO, WHY?
BECAUSE IT HAS NO ODOR
© King Features Syndicate, Inc., 1976.
PEOPLE CAN'T TELL WHEN YOU'VE BEEN DRINKING...
10-28
DIK BROWNE

IF YOU KNOW YOUR RIGHT FROM YOUR LEFT FOOT YOU CAN LEARN TO MARCH...
IF THERE'S ANYBODY WHO DOESN'T KNOW... RAISE YOUR HAND
DIK BROWNE 10-27
© King Features Syndicate, Inc., 1976.
OKAY... WE GOT TROUBLE

IS A VERY FANCY
ESTAURANT
© King Features Syndicate, Inc., 1976.
CHATEAU LA SAUSE '98
VERY GOOD
AND THAT'S JUST THE KETCHUP
10-25 DIK BROWNE